Mama Gets Me Mangoes

By Lydia Meyer

Illustrated by Laura Dalgarno-Platt

© 2017

Mama gets me mangoes every morning, day, and night.
Mama gets me mangoes when the moon is my nightlight.

Mama gets me mangoes when I am tired or sad,
Mama gets me mangoes when I am feeling glad.

Mama gets me mangoes to mash and mush and eat.
Mama gets me mangoes to rub on my sore feet.

Mama Gets Me Mangoes

By Lydia Meyer

Illustrated by Laura Dalgarno-Platt

Mama gets me mangoes as a remedy.
Mama gets me mangoes 'cause she loves me.

But now I get my own mangoes when the buds are in full bloom

'Cause Mama will have a surprise in the month of June.

When I arrive home, Mama has a new baby.
So THAT was the surprise! I thought it would be crazy.

Mama says it's special, It's coming up fast.
'Cause now it is MAY, it's almost in my grasp.

Then one day I'm ready. I know just what to do.
I have to get Mama a mango, the way we always do.

I go down the path, (I've known it for a while)
I come up to that tree after 'bout a mile.

I climb up onto its sturdy branches and limbs.
I look for a juicy one. I pass by all the grim.

I pick one off the branch. It smells so nice and sweet.
Then I pick one for myself, and I begin to eat,

As I eat that Mango, I begin to walk home.
I see how all of the berries have grown.

I pick my Mama lots. She'll like them for lunch.
I walk home again eating one with a CRUNCH!

Mama named her Mica for her black, shining eyes.
And Mama loved my mango; I thought she might cry.

And then, Oh My! Mica clapped and giggled.
It was then I knew that Mica would love mangoes as much as I.

When Mica's grown and older, I'll run when she calls.
I know exactly what to do.

I think I'll bring *her* mangoes!

Lydia Meyer is a fifth grader in Abington, PA. She loves to read, play soccer, and do science experiments. She also plays the violin and the piano and sings in her church's Treble choir. *Mama Gets Me Mangoes* is her first book.

Laura Dalgarno-Platt is originally from Fife in Scotland. She is an artist, illustrator, book lover, movie enthusiast, and general nerd. Since 2013, she has lived in the suburbs of Philadelphia with her husband and four sons.

Made in the USA
Middletown, DE
09 January 2018